THE UN
REVOLUTION

BOOKS BY IAIN H. MURRAY

THE UNDERCOVER
REVOLUTION

*How Fiction Changed
Britain*

Iain H. Murray

THE BANNER OF TRUTH TRUST

THE BANNER OF TRUTH TRUST
3 Murrayfield Road, Edinburgh EH12 6EL, UK
P.O. Box 621, Carlisle, PA 17013, USA

© Iain H. Murray 2009

ISBN-13: 978 1 84871 012 2

Typeset in 11/15 pt Sabon Oldstyle Figures at
the Banner of Truth Trust
Printed in the U.S.A. by
Versa Press, Inc.,
East Peoria, IL

CONTENTS

ILLUSTRATIONS

PREFACE

Several years ago, when spending a few months in Sydney, I was without my own books but near to a good library. That led me to read biographies of several authors whom I had previously known chiefly by their published writings. The outcome of that reading is the present little book.

My theme—the influence of fiction on society—is worthy of much more expansion than I have given to it here. I hope I have said enough to alert others to the importance of what is too commonly overlooked. It is not my belief that the writing of fiction is wrong in itself. John Milton and John Bunyan knew long ago that such writing can serve a moral purpose. Others have since used it to that effect, and there are currently books available to guide the reader to them, for instance, *Invitation to the Classics: A Guide to the Books You've Always Wanted to Read,* edited by Louise Cowan and Os Guinness (Grand Rapids: Baker, 1998). This acknowledgement does not, however, weaken the warning which the following pages contain. Words are powerful things and none can be more injurious than many to be found in fiction. For the reason stated in the second part of the book, I believe the Bible is not fiction. It is given to us as a standard by which we are to judge all things, although, as we seek to do this, we Christians know that our own lives would be utterly condemned by God were it not for his grace freely given to us in Jesus Christ. My hope is that these pages may lead others to the Saviour of the world.

IAIN H. MURRAY

Colinton,
Edinburgh,
August 2008

PART ONE

Evangelical morality was the single most widespread influence in Victorian England. It powerfully influenced the Church of England, was the faith of the Methodists, and revived the older nonconformist sects; it spread through every class and taught simple comprehensible virtues.

Noel Annan,
Leslie Stephen, The Godless Victorian

*Through the long years
I sought peace;
I found ecstasy,
I found anguish,
I found madness,
I found loneliness,
I found the solitary pain
That gnaws the heart,
But peace I did not find.*

Bertrand Russell,
Autobiography

Under the impression that the only proper historical explanation of any event is an evolutionary one, historians have represented the English loss of faith as a gradual stripping away from religion of one dogma after another until nothing remained but the memory of Christianity—the convention of a name and the habit of ritual.

Gertrude Himmelfarb,
Victorian Minds

I

INTRODUCTION

Faith in Christianity is a thing of the past for most people in Britain today. An age of unbelief has returned, with the Bible no longer the authority for personal conduct or social life. Yet it is strange that there should be so little interest in why such a great change has happened.

It is commonly assumed that the reason is well known: namely, that the advance of knowledge in the nineteenth century outdated the traditions and superstitions of former days. The modern man knows too much to accept that he should live according to the Bible.

If this explanation of the change from faith to unbelief is true, one would expect to find documentation for it in history. There must have been a time when real evidence was discovered that made Christianity unbelievable. There must also have been people who, compelled to accept that evidence, promoted the change from the religious to the secular life.

No documentation exists to confirm such an explanation. That there were opinion-makers who changed the climate of thought is not in dispute. But who they were has been too little noticed; and when their lives are examined it will be found that their motivation did not come from new knowledge; it came from something much older than the nineteenth century.

There can be agreement on one thing about the change I will describe: books were the main means by which it came about. Even in the 1840s Thomas Carlyle was claiming that the printed word had changed everything, and that the leaders of the future would be 'the Priesthood of the Writers of Books'. Certainly by faster methods of printing (presses that could produce 18,000 sheets an hour), by paper made from wood pulp, and with an explosion of literacy, books could become what they had never been before.

In the words of Carlyle's biographer, 'No longer did men have to gather round a teacher at a university and learn from him; "The true university these days is a collection of books."[1]

Whose books, then, would secularize the country? Those of Charles Darwin and his popularizer, Thomas Huxley, played a part, but I believe it was a different school of writers that would have the widest influence on late Victorian and Edwardian England. Statistics are significant. In 1870 the largest group of new books to be published was religious. Works of fiction came fifth on the list. With reference to that era, the historian G. M. Trevelyan wrote: 'The popular heroes of that period—and they were true heroes—were religious men first and foremost (Livingstone, Gordon, Lord Shaftesbury, Gladstone).' The minority place that novels had for the reading public in 1870 was in part because evangelical Christianity had little time for them. Hannah More, after achieving celebrity as a playwright, wrote earlier in the century that 'constant familiarity with works of fiction disinclines and disqualifies for active virtues and for spiritual exercises'. She had turned from fiction to writing Christian books of factual narrative or devotion, including *The Shepherd of Salisbury Plain*. William Wilberforce was reflecting the evangelical

[1] Simon Heffer, *Moral Desperado, A Life of Thomas Carlyle* (London: Weidenfeld and Nicholson, 1995), p. 168.

attitude when he referred to that title in the words:

> I am always sorry that the Waverley novels [of Sir
> Walter Scott] should have so little moral or relig-
> ious object. They remind me of a giant spending his
> strength in cracking nuts. I would rather go to render
> my account at the last day, carrying with me *The
> Shepherd of Salisbury Plain,* than bearing a load of
> these volumes, full as they are of genius.

Sixteen years after 1870, however, in 1886, a
further census on popular literature put works of
fiction at the head of the list. The following year
Robert Louis Stevenson felt able to assert, 'The most
influential books, and the truest in their influence, are
works of fiction.'[2] The reading habits of the nation
were entering a new era and the type of literature
that was to have the most pervasive influence upon
the twentieth century was the work of novelists and
dramatists.

A most potent attack on Christianity in modern
times has been little recognized. Most of the writers
to whom I will refer used fiction to present something

---

[2] Writing on 'Books Which Influenced Me,' in the *British
Weekly,* 1887. To give references to all the quotations that follow
in the next chapter would greatly overload the pages. For the
most part I will restrict references to the titles of the books I have
been using, rather than every quotation from these books.

they believed to be better than the Christian life. Their presentations were to become the accepted wisdom of succeeding generations and they have powerfully affected society down to the present day. Yet it can be shown that their motivation did not spring from the finding of something better; it came rather from a dislike of the evangelical truth which most of them knew in their childhood. I shall argue that their claim to have arrived at a better knowledge, when tested by the evidence of their lives (now fully documented by many biographers), will be found to be fraudulent. The truth is that it is unbelief rather than Christianity that depends upon the irrational for its survival.

Robert Louis Stevenson
with his father, Thomas

2

ROBERT LOUIS STEVENSON

Robert Louis Stevenson came early into my life when his *Treasure Island* held my attention while most other books failed. My interest in him deepened in later years when a move to Colinton, Edinburgh, brought us into a district once very familiar to RLS.

If our first Scottish home did not stand on what was once the glebe of his grandfather, the Rev. Lewis Balfour, it was very close to it. The Colinton manse, beside the church where Balfour spent, in his words, 'a goodly part of eighty years', was in close proximity to us. One of Balfour's daughters, Margaret, married Thomas Stevenson, and in 1850 their only child, Robert Louis, was born. For the first ten years of his life Louis was often at the Colinton manse. Beside that manse was the Water of Leith, with its snuff and paper mills, and only a water door separated the manse garden from that river. On the slope beyond were the homes of Colinton village upon which the Pentland Hills looked down. This was a scene that dominated Stevenson's childhood and which we also came to know so well.

The Stevensons' own home was five miles away in the Edinburgh New Town, and the Christian influence was no less evident there than it was at the Colinton manse. Louis's father, a distinguished civil engineer, came from a decided Christian family. Famous for his work with lighthouses, he was, as his son would later describe him, one 'by whose devices the great sea lights in every quarter of the world now shine more brightly'.

As a nurse for Louis, the Stevensons appointed Alison Cunningham, a young woman of definite belief and Christian commitment. While the parents went to St Stephen's Church of Scotland, she attended the ministry of W. G. Blaikie in a Free Church congregation. 'Cummy', as Alison was called, came to be the boy's governess and virtually a second mother. She was no dull teacher, and Louis revelled in her stories so much that he scarcely began to read for himself until he was eight. At the head of Cummy's subjects for her pupil were the Bible, the *Shorter Catechism*, hymns, and, sometimes, the writings of Robert Murray M'Cheyne.

In a sense, this was a 'covenanting childhood', and out of it came Louis's first small book, *The Pentland Rising*, written in 1866 when he was sixteen, and published by the aid of an admiring father. It commemorated, in careful detail, the failed attempt of the Covenanters to defeat the forces of Charles II in a battle close to Colinton in 1666. The youthful commitment of the author to the side of the losers was clear. He complained, 'It is the fashion of the day to jeer and to mock, to execrate and condemn, the noble band of Covenanters.'

In 1867, the year after this publication, RLS entered Edinburgh University. In his later exaggerated words, he was then, 'lean, idle, ugly, unpopular'. Certainly he was a loner at first, in part the result of his sheltered early years. As an only child he had been idolized by his mother. But before long he found a new world, different from his affluent home and the respectable Presbyterian standards which characterized much of Edinburgh. There were easy-going companions to enjoy among his fellow-students; public houses to visit — 'frequented', he later wrote, 'by the lowest order of prostitutes';[3] and books to read that he could never have seen in his father's study. At times he hung around Greyfriars churchyard for hours at a time, reading Baudelaire, an author who 'would have corrupted St Paul'. Of all this his parents knew nothing, and the young Stevenson became a man of two lives. With like-minded friends at the university, he formed a frivolous club that had for one of its rules, 'Ignore everything that our parents taught us.' When his father happened on a piece of paper recording these words, and questioned Louis, he was shocked to discover his son no longer believed in the Christian religion. The date was January 31, 1873, and the father's verdict, 'You have rendered my whole life a failure.' A sorrow came into the life of Thomas Stevenson that was to remain until his death.

The same year, 1873, was to be a turning point in RLS's life in another respect. In July his parents urged him to take a holiday in the home of his mother's niece in Suffolk, where he had been before. The niece

[3] *Letters of Robert Louis Stevenson*, eds. B. A. Booth and E. Mehew, vol. 1 (New Haven: Yale University Press, 1994), p. 210. The first edition of *Letters of Robert Louis Stevenson*, ed. Sidney Colvin, vol. 1 (London: Methuen, 1899) contains letters abridged and expurgated, whereas they will be found in full in the Yale edition which runs into eight volumes.

was married to an English clergyman, and perhaps the Stevensons hoped that Louis would be helped by such company. It was not to be. The twenty-two-year-old Scot spent most of the time, not with his relatives, but with another house guest, Frances Sitwell. Separated from her own clergyman husband, Mrs Sitwell dazzled RLS by her beauty, her vitality, and her literary interests. She at once became his chief confidant; if she did not actually encourage romance, she did nothing to stop an infatuation on his part. Judging by his many letters to her after his return to Edinburgh, she had no more Christianity than he had. 'I believe in you as others believe in the Bible', he wrote to her. And for her sympathy he freely shared all his family news: 'It was really pathetic to hear my father praying pointedly for me today at family worship, and to think the poor man's supplications were addressed to nothing better able to hear and answer than the chandelier.'[4]

Until this point, apart from his small book, RLS had written only for university papers and for local theatricals. It was Frances Sitwell who saw he had talent to reach far wider circles. She enthused about the 'young genius' from Edinburgh to her close friend

---

[4] *Letters* (Yale), vol.1, p.302.

Sidney Colvin, and arranged for the two to meet. Colvin, an editor and literary critic in London, was well placed to open the door for RLS into the capital's literary world. He proposed him for the Savile Club where the Scot met men who played a large part in his future. One of them was Leslie Stephen, earlier ordained in the Church of England but now set on a different career as editor of the monthly *Cornhill Magazine* which had no religious content. Stephen's extensive writings would include *An Agnostic's Apology and Other Essays*. His biographer believed, 'He was the first Englishman to consider the novel as seriously as the critics had treated poetry at a time when novels were still dismissed as light entertainment.'[5] The writing of many authors, including RLS's, began in monthly serial form under Stephen's guidance. Speaking of his debt to the *Cornhill*, RLS would later write, 'I was received there in the very best of society, and under the eye of the very best of editors.'

Another young author writing for Leslie Stephen was W. E. Henley, whom Stephen introduced to RLS in 1875. That same year Henley wrote his best-known poem, 'Invictus', and RLS was quick to quote it:

[5] Noel Annan, *Leslie Stephen, The Godless Victorian* (London: Weidenfeld and Nicholson, 1984), p. 317.

Out of the night that covers me,
  Black as the Pit from pole to pole,
I thank whatever gods may be
  For my unconquerable soul . . .

It matters not how strait the gate,
  How charged with punishments the scroll,
I am the master of my fate:
  I am the captain of my soul.

Henley became RLS's close friend and literary agent. Of similar significance for RLS's future life was Edmund Gosse, whom he met at the Savile Club. Perhaps it was a joke when Charles Baxter said it was Gosse 'who has led the poor dear young man astray'. The truth was they were all now taken up with the glamour of a literary circle which, as Gosse's father had warned him, was 'utterly alien from Christ'.[6] A poet, reviewer and author, Gosse was ultimately knighted in 1925. When Cummy met Gosse on a visit to the North her first impression was favourable. She was impressed by the way he read the Bible at family prayers and told Stevenson: 'He's the only one of your fine friends who can do justice to

---

[6] Ann Thwaite, *Glimpses of the Wonderful: The Life of Philip Henry Gosse 1810-1888* (London: Faber, 2002), p. 288. On Philip Gosse, see also J. Rendle-Short, *Green Eye of the Storm* (Edinburgh: Banner of Truth, 1998), pp. 1–48.

the Word of God.' Little did she know how he and Louis could joke over immorality together. In some striking respects the lives of the two men ran parallel. Gosse, one year older than RLS, had also been brought up as an only child in a Bible-believing home, and turned to a literary career while abandoning the faith of his father. If RLS's rejection of Christianity would remain largely recorded in his personal letters, Gosse's break with his father was to be explained to the world in his much-acclaimed book, *Father and Son*. Although focused on his family estrangement, this book was in fact an *apologia* for the whole movement to unbelief. Gosse saw himself as a leader in a new epoch. While his father 'was born to fly backward', he 'could not help being carried forward'. In the Preface, he professed to be writing 'the diagnosis of a dying Puritanism'. The break with his father was not really his father's fault, he explained; the real blame belonged to the evangelical Christianity to which the father adhered:

> What a charming companion, what a delightful parent, what a courteous and engaging friend my Father would have been, and would pre-eminently have been to me, if it had not been for this stringent piety which ruined it all. Let me speak plainly. After my long experience, after my patience and forbearance,

I have surely the right to protest against the untruth (would that I could apply to it any other word!) that evangelical religion, or any religion in a violent form, is a wholesome or desirable adjunct to human life. It divides heart from heart . . . it invents virtues which are sterile and cruel; it invents sins which are no sins at all, but which darken the heaven of innocent joy with futile clouds of remorse.[7]

Thus, in the mid-1870s, the direction for RLS's career was set. His father's first hope had been that he would join his own engineering business. When there was no prospect of that being fulfilled, RLS was encouraged to take a law degree in Edinburgh with the promise of £1,000 on its completion. That promise was kept in 1874, but the parents had to accept that their son was determined to be an author not a lawyer. He would need financial support for many years to come; yet sorrow over his unbelief did not lessen their kindness. RLS was always welcomed home, even after he had told Sitwell, 'I am simply incapable of cohabiting any house with my father.' If he was at home on a Sunday, he would sit alone in

---

[7] Edmund Gosse, *Father and Son: A Study in Two Temperaments* (London: Heinemann, 1909), p. 329. The first edition went through four printings in six months. The second edition of 1909 had a second printing within the year.

his room, reporting that 'the whole life of Edinburgh has been sucked into pious edifices.' In 1876, while travelling purportedly in the interest of his poor health, he transferred his affection to another woman, Fanny Osbourne, whom he met in France. The fact that she was already married did not hinder their intimacy, and after she returned to California and to her husband, he followed her. When she divorced, he married her in 1880. RLS's father, far off in Scotland and helpless to prevent what he could not approve, promised an annual allowance of £250, not a small figure for those times.

My purpose here is not to give an account of RLS.[8] In brief the 1880s were to see him rise to fame as magazine articles were followed by books, with *Treasure Island* the first in 1881. From the pages of that book one could suppose the author was a carefree storyteller for boys, and certainly some of his books were no more than exciting adventures. But the reality of his personal life was different. With Fanny, and her son, he moved from place to place,

[8] There are numerous biographies; the best of modern ones known to me are those of James Pope Hennessy, *Robert Louis Stevenson* (London: Jonathan Cape, 1974), and Claire Harman, *Robert Louis Stevenson, A Biography* (London; Harper Collins, 2005). Exact biographical detail will be found in the Yale edition of his *Letters*.

his health and his recurring depressions unhelped by alcohol. When a doctor in Nice warned him to give up drink, he wrote of himself in language meant to amuse a friend:

> Of that lean, feverish, voluble and whiskyfied young Scot, who once sparked through France and Britain, bent on art and the pleasures of the flesh, there now remains no quality but the strong language. That, at least, I shall take gravewards: my last word, it's like, will be an execration.

Even the gift of a house in Bournemouth from his father did not settle the couple. The advanced illness of Thomas Stevenson, followed by his death, brought RLS back to Edinburgh for the last time in May 1887. He was too late for his father to recognize him. Louis arranged the funeral, with some details already settled by his father. For the graveside Thomas Stevenson had left a short letter to be read. But the weather that morning was bad, and his much-loved son, anxious for his own health, left the proceedings before he could hear it. The next year RLS and Fanny sailed for the South Seas, where they made a home on Vailima in the Samoan Islands. There he died suddenly, aged 44, of a cerebral haemorrhage in 1894, his writing broken off in the middle of a sentence. He hated

'growing old'; and some of his most poignant verses
take us back to the manse garden at Colinton,

> The river, on from mill to mill,
>   Flows past our childhood's garden still;
> But ah! We children never more
>   Shall watch it from the water door!
>
> The eternal dawn, beyond a doubt,
>   Shall break on hill and plain,
> And put all stars and candles out,
>   Ere we be young again.

Had he died young, RLS once said, a tract would
have been written on his childhood piety. As it was,
he lived, 'kicking against the pricks of civilization,
scoffing at the dogmatism in every creed, especially
the one he had been reared in'.[9] For him, 'the eternal
dawn' existed only in poetry. 'If I could believe in the
immortality business', he wrote to a friend in 1886,
'the world would indeed be too good to be true; but
. . . the sods cover us, and the worm that never dies,
the conscience sleeps well at last.' Life was only a
'pilgrimage from nothing to nowhere'. The *Shorter
Catechism* he could quote by heart, and occasionally
praise its opening question, but it 'was not the merri-

---

[9] E. Blantyre Simpson, *Robert Louis Stevenson's Edinburgh
Days* (London: Hodder and Stoughton, 1898), p.131.

est epitome of religion', only a 'dry-as-dust epitome'. When the contents for a collected edition of his works were being discussed in 1894, he wrote to Colvin, 'I heartily abominate and reject the idea of reprinting 'The Pentland Rising'. For God's sake let me be buried first.'

* * * * *

How is the change that marked RLS's life to be explained? Part of his own explanation had to do with the character of Christians as he considered them to be—too often joyless people, spending grim Sundays with dull books and no fiction. Not that he would accuse Cummy in such terms, and the picture is muted when applied to his father (he was 'morbid' and given to 'melancholy'); but believers in the Bible in general were the target for criticism. His father's mother, he tells us, was 'a devout, unambitious woman, occupied with her Bible, her children, and her house; easily shocked, and associating largely with a clique of godly parasites'. Her husband, he implies, suffered her bigotry for the sake of peace. His maternal grandfather at Colinton was capable of kindness but he was a grave, awesome figure. 'When sent in to say a psalm to my grandfather, I went in quaking with fear', he professed to recall. On another occasion, at the Colinton manse, he was once enjoying reading the *Arabian Nights* 'when my clergyman grandfather (a man we counted pretty stiff) came in behind me. I grew blind with terror; but instead of ordering the book away he said he envied me. Ah! well he might.'[10]

RLS knew how to use language to create the impression he wished to make. When he tells us elsewhere that this grandfather, supposedly so hostile to fiction, 'was a great lover of Shakespeare', we begin to doubt the accuracy of his other words. One who knew the Stevenson family, commented of the son, 'He judged his father and everyone who did not agree with him as bigoted.'[11] RLS's descriptions of Christians as a defence of his unbelief are unconvincing.

Undoubtedly RLS and Edmund Gosse would have commiserated with one another on their 'unfortunate' childhoods. The latter's father, Philip Henry Gosse was to be remembered, not by his writings, but as the narrow man of 'morbid conscience', portrayed in *Father and Son*. Only in recent times has it been established 'just how unreliable a witness Edmund is'.[12] Philip Gosse's pleadings with his son are very

---

[10] Most of these family descriptions will be found in his book *Memories and Portraits*.

[11] Simpson, *Edinburgh Days*, p. 50.

[12] Thwaite, *Glimpses*, p. xvi. Thwaite makes full use of evidence

similar to those of RLS's father. He wrote to him: 'You say that you have a right to think for yourself . . . Of course . . . but have I not a right to counsel, to suggest, to entreat if I see you choosing fatal error . . . Have I not a right to grieve?'[13]

Thomas Stevenson had a different understanding of the change in his son. He put it down to the authors he read and the company he kept. The particular writer that damaged Louis, he believed, was Herbert Spencer, who had applied the theory of evolution to religion and philosophy. According to this thinking, man is not fallen from an original perfection; rather he is advancing towards it. Certainly RLS acknowledged, 'I came under the influence of Herbert Spencer. No more persuasive rabbi exists, and few better.'

But Thomas Stevenson was right also on the influence of his son's companions. While still a student,

---

from those who knew the father, e.g, Arthur Hunt, 'Mr Edmund Gosse's portrait of his father gives a totally wrong impression of the man' (p. 292). An observation in the *British and Foreign Evangelical Review*, vol. 1 (Edinburgh: Johnstone and Hunter, 1852), pp.102–3, is often true: 'There are none who speak and write so bitterly against evangelical piety, as do apostate children; those who remember the wounds but not the balm—who were convinced but not converted.'

[13] Thwaite, *Glimpses*, pp. 276-7.

Louis's circle of boon companions—Bob Stevenson (his cousin), William Walter Ferrier, and Charles Baxter—were all of one spirit: 'heartless drunken young dogs we were', RLS wrote to Baxter years later. Yet Thomas Stevenson did not simply blame others. His pain was the greater because he knew his son was not an innocent party. In a letter to Sitwell, RLS summarized what his father said to him during a scene which occurred in September 1873:

> A poor end for all my tenderness . . . I have made all my life to suit you—I have worked for you and gone out of my way for you—and the end of it is that I find you in opposition to the Lord Jesus Christ—I find everything gone—I would ten times sooner have seen you lying in your grave than that you should be shaking the faith of other young men.[14]

As already said, RLS was not at his father's graveside in 1887 to hear the letter the deceased had appointed to be read. But he knew the contents; and, while there is no evidence they came back to

[14] *Letters* (Yale), vol. 1, p. 312. Hennessy says that RLS would 'agonize over what he was making his parents suffer . . . but he would re-assure himself that it was their rigid minds and their bourgeois attitudes that were causative and fundamentally to blame.' As late as 1885 Thomas Stevenson was still supporting his son financially. 'It is fortunate for me I have a father', RLS wrote that year, 'or I should long ago have died.'

him in the far-off Pacific, one cannot but hope that they did:

17 Heriot Row,
Edinburgh

May I be allowed to say very humbly—God knows how humbly—that, believing in Christ, I confidently trust I shall not be disowned by Him when the last trumpet shall sound.

My good friends! I hope our friendship is not ended, but only for a time interrupted, and that we may all meet again in that better land which has been prepared for us by our Father and our Saviour, the blessed passport to which has been freely offered to all. Amen.

THOMAS STEVENSON

This I desire to be read at my funeral.[15]

---

[15] Simpson, *Edinburgh Days*, pp. 52–3. After the death of RLS, his wife published *Prayers Written at Vailima, by Robert Louis Stevenson* (London; Chatto & Windus, 2008). The nature of these prayers, and her own Introduction, give no evidence that he trusted in Christ as his father did.

Thomas Hardy,
aged 30, c. 1870.

3

THOMAS HARDY

In December 1839 Thomas Hardy, the father of the novelist, brought his bride, Jemima Hand, to the rambling cottage some three miles from Dorchester which had belonged to the family since 1801. While a small builder's business, also inherited, kept him above the poverty that many of the country people of Dorset then suffered, the Hardy family had known better times. It seems the rural location had inspired neither ambition nor commercial success. In the life of their only son, born in 1840 and named after his father, the position would be different. At the death of the son in 1928 there would be a two-column obituary in *The Times* and the comment that English literature had lost 'its most eminent figure'.

The Hardys belonged to the parish of Stinsford and would be seen in the church there every Sunday. Yet it was the adjoining parish of Fordington that came to have a greater influence on the son of Thomas and Jemima. This was because Henry Moule, vicar of Fordington since 1829, was above the normal run of parish priests. Jemima had first heard him preach as a girl of fifteen and his reputation had only risen through the years. In the last great plague of cholera in the area, Moule had defied all personal danger both in visiting the sick and dying and in organizing the cleansing of homes of the bereaved. When Moule's fragrant ministry at last ended in 1880, Thomas Hardy Jr. wrote to one of the Moule sons:

> Though not, topographically, a parishioner of your father's I virtually stood in that relation to him, and his home generally, during many years of my life, and I always feel precisely as if I had been one.[16]

Hardy's link with the Fordington vicarage was in part through the progress of his education. After a short time in a village school, his parents surprised

[16] Florence E. Hardy, *The Early Life of Thomas Hardy,* (New York: Macmillan, 1928), p. 176. This volume was the first of a two-volume work, prepared by Hardy himself as far as the year 1918, but published as biography under the name of his second wife. In reality the work was thus largely autobiography although written in the third person.

28

some by sending him to a Nonconformist school in Dorchester on account of the known ability of its teacher. Among much else, the ten commandments and some of Isaac Watts' hymns were learnt by heart, and such was his progress in Latin that before he left school at the age of sixteen he won a pocket edition of Beza's *Latin New Testament*. A love for books born in him at this time was to be lifelong, and it competed with the career he began at the age of sixteen as an apprentice to an architect. He now took up the study of Greek, with the principal object of studying the New Testament in the orginal. Another apprentice, Henry Bastow, was equally eager, and after work 'it became an occasional practice for the youths to take out their Testaments into the fields and sit on a gate reading them.'[17] It seems that Hardy's main encourager in the study of Greek and in other literary pursuits was Horace Moule, the fourth son of the vicar of Fordington. Eight years Hardy's senior, Horace had studied (without completion) at Oxford and Cambridge. 'Handsome, charming, cultivated, scholarly', his impact on the younger man is said to have been 'immense'.[18]

[17] Ibid., p. 40.
[18] *Thomas Hardy, A Biography*, Michael Millgate (New York: Random House, 1982), p. 67. I am indebted to Professor Millgate for much of my information.

This close contact with the Fordington vicarage was certainly established by 1857, two years before an evident movement of the Spirit of God brought an awakening to the parish. Handley Moule said of the event:

> Surely it was divine. No artificial means of excitement were dreamt of; my Father's whole genius was against it. No powerful personality, no Moody or Aitken, came to us. A city-missionary and a London bible–woman were the only helpers from a distance . . . Up and down the village the pastor, the pastoress, and their faithful helpers, as they went their daily rounds, found 'the anxious'. And the church was thronged to overflowing, and so was the spacious school-room, night after night throughout the week. The very simplest means carried with them a heavenly power. The plain reading of a chapter often conveyed the call of God to men and women, and they 'came to Jesus as they were'. I do not think I exaggerate when I say that hundreds of people at that time were awakened, awed, made conscious of eternal realities. And a goodly number of these shewed in all their after life that they were indeed new creatures.[19]

---

[19] Handley C. G. Moule, *Memories of a Vicarage* (London: RTS, 1913), pp. 49-50.

Hardy must have seen and felt this revival and we do not doubt that it was related to Homer and Virgil being 'thrown aside' for Scripture. And this stirring of his soul was not only through his friends in the Church of England. His fellow apprentice, Henry Bastow, was a Nonconformist who was baptized as a believer in September 1858. This led to Hardy meeting Frederick Perkins, the Baptist minister in Dorchester, and his sons, of whom he writes: 'They formed an austere and frugal household, and won his admiration by their thoroughness and strenuousness.' Bastow's hope was that Hardy had been 'won' to Christ himself, later recalling, 'he once professed to love a crucified Saviour'. In his Bible Hardy noted the date 'April 17th/61' against the passage Ephesians 5:8–24, which begins, 'For ye were sometimes darkness, but now are light in the Lord'.[20]

The apprentice architect, however, was not to be among those who showed in later life that they were real Christians. Within a few years his association with 'earnest' evangelicals had passed. Bastow left Dorchester for Tasmania, and Hardy, at the age of twenty-two, for London in 1862. In what amounted to his own autobiography, he would later write that

[20] Florence E. Hardy, *Early Life*, p. 41.

after his friend's departure 'and the weakening of his influence, Hardy, like St Augustine, lapsed from the Greek New Testament back again to pagan writers'.[21] There were other distractions. Ever susceptible to feminine attractions, he was now virtually engaged to Eliza Nicholls. It was her departure for a post in London that prompted Hardy to follow, although he took the precaution of buying a return rail ticket in case he found no work or lodgings. In the event he quickly settled in Kilburn (north London) and gained a place in the offices of an architect.

Before long Hardy's commitment to architecture dwindled, as did his affection for Eliza. For one thing, her Christianity was now too definite for him. An introduction to theatres and operas had begun to prove more exciting than the life he had known with her in Dorchester. In far-off Tasmania Bastow sensed the difference, and urged in letters, 'Don't you dear Brother forget our little meetings together at our place of assignation—and oh do let Jesus have the very best of all your time and thought.' Again: 'Dear old Tom don't you let your eye get off Jesus—I did hear a whisper that you had begun to think that works may do something in the way of salvation—but dear

---

[21] This seems to be a misconception since Augustine's knowledge of Greek was quite limited, and there is no question of his lapsing to the study of pagan writers

fellow if you think so — don't oh don't for a moment let it prevent your leaning for all your salvation on "Him".'[22] Hardy's change was gradual and there was no sudden giving up of church attendance and Bible reading, particularly as 'the Church' figured in his plans for the future. His love of books had brought an ambition to be an author, and the best hope of success seemed to be settlement in a country parsonage where he could pursue a quiet literary life. This was still his goal up to 1866 when information from Horace Moule on the university preparation he would need closed the door to Cambridge. It was just as well, for his biographer writes: 'By 1866 Hardy's views had greatly changed; he no longer accepted many of the Church's doctrinal positions.'

It is beyond my present purpose to discuss what had brought this change of belief. The opinions of liberal theology in *Essays and Reviews* had impressed him. So had the agnosticism of Thomas Huxley, and he was 'charmed' by the poetry of another avowed non-Christian, Algernon Charles Swinburne.[23] As

---

[22] Millgate, pp. 64–5. Hardy's letters to Bastow have not survived.

[23] In 1865 Hardy was reading J. S. Mill and Auguste Comte. It would appear that, despite his background, the influence of Horace Moule was not beneficial. He was not the same kind of man as his father and his brother, Handley Moule.

far as his future career was concerned it gradually became clear to him that if it was to be that of a writer he would need to find his own means of support. A first short piece had been accepted from his pen for publication in 1865. In 1871, not without difficulty, he had his first novel accepted by a publisher. It was followed, the same year, by *Under the Greenwood Tree*. Both titles appeared anonymously. They drew the attention of Leslie Stephen, educated at Eton and Cambridge and editor of the *Cornhill*, whom we have already noticed in connection with the launching of Stevenson's literary career. A letter from Stephen, with an invitation to write for the *Cornhill*, was to decide Hardy's future and establish him as a novelist. With enough money to live on now coming in, architecture was given up, and for the rest of his days he would be among the new literary set that changed novel writing from a dubious to a profitable career.

Like Stevenson, Hardy joined the Savile Club and came to number Edmund Gosse and his circle among his friends. His link with Leslie Stephen was more than merely literary. In Hardy's own words, Stephen's 'philosophy would influence his own for many years, indeed, more than that of any other contemporary'.[24] It was Stephen who did so much to promote Huxley's

[24] Florence E. Hardy, *Early Life*, p. 132.

newly coined term 'agnosticism' — the consequence, it was supposed, of the 'proof' of evolution supplied by Darwin. But as Gertrude Himmelfarb has perceptively written, the widespread acceptance of the new teaching was not due to Darwin at all:

> Many of the young agnostics regarded it not as a new and upsetting revelation but rather as an old and obvious truth. Stephen was one of those to whom agnosticism was as old and obvious as common sense. It was, to quote the title of one of his essays in his *An Agnostic's Apology*, 'The Religion of All Sensible Men'.[25]

In more accurate language, unbelief suits human nature.

When Stephen finally renounced his status as a clergyman in 1875, it was Hardy he asked to witness the deed of renunciation. As Stephen explained the need for the deed to Hardy, the latter remembered:

> He said grimly that he was really a reverend gentleman still, little as he might look it, and that he thought it as well to cut himself adrift of a calling for which, to say the least, he had always been utterly unfit. The deed was executed with due formality. Our conversation then turned upon theologies decayed

---

[25] G. Himmelfarb, *Victorian Minds* (Chicago: Ivan Dee, 1995), p. 206.

and defunct, the origin of things, the constitution of matter, the unreality of time, and kindred subjects. He told me he had 'wasted' much time on systems of religion . . .

Hardy became one of the leaders in a new style of novel writing. Instead of moralizing in conformity with accepted norms of behaviour, he aimed at 'realism'. Thackeray had already done this with his aim of a 'truthful representation of actual life', but Hardy carried it further as he concentrated on 'the immortal puzzle'—the relationship between men and women, their happy meetings, dissatisfied lives and sad partings. For his scenery he used the rustic life of the Dorset that he knew so well, renaming it 'Wessex'. The aim in good novel writing, he once noted, 'is to give pleasure by gratifying the love of the uncommon', while depicting characters as normal and ordinary.

What was 'normal' was soon a focus of dispute in the controversy his books caused. Edmund Gosse assured him: 'Your books are very important to me. I look upon you as without approach the best English novelist living.' Publishers did not all share that view. In turning down a manuscript from him, the editor of *Macmillan's Magazine* concluded that, while the nature of the material would 'no doubt bring it

plenty of praise', he was 'rather too old-fashioned—
as I suppose I must call it—to quite relish the entirely
modern style of fiction'. Nervous of the inclusion of
items 'not suitable for family reading', Hardy's publishers repeatedly sought to censor and edit what he
wrote. This did not allay the criticism of reviewers
which came to a head with the publication of his *Tess
of the d'Urbervilles*. The *Saturday Review* disliked
the prominence given to Tess's sexual attractions and
concluded that Hardy had told 'an unpleasant story
in an unpleasant way'. The morality of the book was
widely condemned. A reviewer in the *London World*
would later write: 'Of all forms of sex-mania in fiction we have no hesitation in pronouncing the most
unpleasant to be the Wessex-mania of Mr Thomas
Hardy.'

Michael Millgate, Hardy's biographer, represents
the novelist as puzzled at the extent of the opposition
he encountered. 'Throughout his career he seems to
have been repeatedly astonished at the response made
to his work first by editors and then by reviewers.'[26]
It is hard to credit Hardy's sincerity in this regard. He
sought to represent his critics as 'prudes' and 'Mrs
Grundys', but he knew very well that the attitudes

[26] Millgate, p. 371.

he was promoting were fundamentally at variance with the Christianity still so widely accepted in the country. Certainly there were times when he spoke as though it was only the beliefs, not the morality of Christianity, that he opposed. He 'had a dream' that the Church might become 'an undogmatical, non-theological establishment for the promotion of virtuous living on which all honest men are agreed'.[27] But in truth he knew there was no agreement on the meaning of 'virtuous living'. Christianity 'he saw as persistently hostile to morality'.[28] Despite being 'so roundly abused by the press', he said, 'I am deter-mined—to exhibit what I feel ought to be exhibited about life, to show that what we call immorality, irreligion, &c, are often true morality, true religion.' Included in this 'true morality' was his opposition to the evils of marriage and the marriage laws.

Hardy once asserted that what he wrote and his own life were indivisible, and it is certainly true that the substance of his material was drawn very largely from his experience, and particularly from his relat-ionships with women. It is in his personal life that the key to understanding him lies. The pessimism and tragedy of his novels came directly from his

[27] Ibid., p. 247.
[28] Ibid., p. 372.

life. I have already referred to his break with Eliza Nicholls; the explanation in that case including his preference for her sister. This second infatuation was then replaced by one for Cassie Pole, for whom, it is believed, he bought a ring. But she also was to be jilted as yet another woman intervened. He met Emma Gifford in Cornwall in 1870, and, after hesitation, married her in 1874, at the outset of his career as an author. The marriage lasted until Emma's death in 1912, although in a real sense it had ended many years earlier.

When Hardy wrote of individuals 'shut into marriages' with the wrong person, it was an expression of self-pity. His friends, ready to please him, spoke of their sympathy for him when they met Emma, but in reality it was Emma who chiefly deserved sympathy, not least when she saw obvious references to their loveless marriage on the pages of her husband's novels. Hardy, she confided to a friend, wrote 'to please . . . others! or himself—but not me.' He was 'a great writer, but not a great man'. 'He understands only the women he invents—the others not at all.' Long before Emma's death, Hardy was hunting other women, one of whom, Florence Dugdale, he would write to as 'Dearest Florence' and subsequently marry.

At the deepest level, the difference between Emma and Thomas Hardy appears to have been over Christian commitment. He would describe himself as 'a harmless agnostic' and allege, questionably perhaps, that when he first met Emma she was the same. Whether this was true or not, it is clear that at a later date Mrs Hardy was a definite evangelical Christian, and had no sympathy for the 'blank materialism' in her husband's writings. To one of his friends, Edward Clodd, author of *Pioneers of Evolution,* she wrote: 'The chapters I greatly object to, are those with which you seem to have taken so much pains to say—There is no God—There is no Christ.'

Hardy instead of being 'a harmless agnostic' was clearly hostile to the Christian revelation of God. This comes out plainly in the poetry which he published in the second half of his career, when tired of being 'shot at' for his novels. The extent to which he speaks of 'God' in his poems is surprising, yet it is a 'God' who can say of the world,

> It lost my interest from the first,
> My aims therefor succeeding ill . . .[29]

---

[29] 'God-Forgotten', in *The Collected Poems of Thomas Hardy* (London: Macmillan, 1962), p. 112. The fourth edition of this volume was published in 1930. The same tone recurs in several other poems, e.g. 'God's Education'.

In his poem 'God's Funeral' there is a touch of autobiography as he describes those gathered at the imagined event,

> Some in the background then I saw,
> Sweet women, youths, men, all incredulous
> Who chimed: 'This is a counterfeit of straw!'. . .
> I could not buoy their faith: and yet
> Many I had known: with all I sympathized;
> And though struck speechless, I did not forget
> That what was mourned for, I, too, once had
>   prized.

Another poem begins,

> Since Reverend Doctors now declare
> That clerks and people must prepare
> To doubt if Adam ever were . . .

And concludes,

> All churchgoing will I forswear,
> And sit on Sundays in my chair,
> And read that moderate man Voltaire.[30]

It would be a mistake to read into such lines any wish for a recovery of what he had given up. For Hardy, God was 'fate'—a power without feeling or

---

[30] 'The Respectable Burgher on "The Higher Criticism"', Ibid., pp. 146–7.

purpose. When referring on one occasion to 'a charming young lady' he had known, he told a friend he would have married her 'but for a stupid blunder of God Almighty'. Given such words, it is not surprising that he was ready to write blasphemy concerning the birth of Christ. He was bitter in his belief that the poem 'God's Funeral' was the reason why he was not appointed Poet Laureate in 1913. 'It was enough', he wrote to Gosse, 'to damn me for the Laureateship . . . Fancy Nonconformity on the one hand & Oxford on the other, pouring out their vials on Mr Asquith for such an enormity.' Yet the disapproval was by no means universal; that same year Hardy was given the honorary degree of D.Litt. at Cambridge.

One of the strangest turns in Hardy's life followed the death of Emma in 1912. An initial relief at being able to marry Florence Dugdale, thirty-eight years his junior, very quickly gave way to an enduring remorse at the way he had treated his first wife. Florence, who was well acquainted with his previous marital dissatisfaction, was now astonished to find him writing with so much regret of the wife whose memory he now idolized in verse. In the comment of Millgate,

> For Florence Dugdale, Hardy's obsession with his dead wife was both painful and bewildering. Painful because she knew from first-hand experience what

his later years with Emma had been like—she once said that Hardy and Emma had been in the midst of a violent quarrel in November 1912 [the month of Emma's death] and about to separate.[31]

A number of Hardy's poems, published at this time under the title *Satires of Circumstance*, were now on Emma. Florence, even in the very year of her marriage, could refer to another man as 'the only person who ever loved me'. Her resentment was as understandable as Emma's had formerly been. It is not surprising that Lytton Strachey described the book of poems as 'the melancholy of regretful recollection, of bitter speculation, of immortal longings unsatisfied; it is the melancholy of one who has suffered, in Gibbon's poignant phrase, "the abridgement of hope".' Florence took from the book the impression that the author's second marriage was 'a most disastrous one & that his sole wish is to find refuge in the grave with her with whom he alone found happiness'.

The truth was that Hardy's second wife was experiencing the same self-absorbed and self-seeking man that her predecessor had suffered. Hardy's remorse was a result of his guilt and self-pity. He was the unhappy victim of the 'circumstances' that were

[31] Millgate, *Hardy,* pp. 489-90.

against him. He professed to believe that 'human beings are of no matter or appreciable importance in this nonchalant universe', but his memories of Emma were inconsistent with that belief. Nor did he recognize that the tragedies of his life, reflected in those of which he wrote, were of his own making. When he died on January 11, 1928, his last sudden words to a nurse beside him were, 'Eva, what is this?'

By that date much in the national mood was already changing. Dressed in his doctoral robe after his death, Thomas Hardy was cremated and his ashes buried in Westminster Abbey. He was the first of the new school of fiction writers to be so honoured. The last novelist to be buried there had been Charles Dickens in 1870. In a comment on the obsequies at the Abbey on January 16, 1928, T. E. Lawrence wrote to a friend:

> I regret Hardy's funeral service. So little of it suited the old man's nature. He would have smiled, tolerantly, at it all; but I grow indignant for him, knowing that these sleek Deans and Canons were acting a lie behind his name. Hardy was too great to be suffered as an enemy of their faith: so he must be redeemed.

'Redeemed' he was, and numbers of us had to read him as school boys in the 1940s, at least in an 'edited' version.

We leave the last word with Hardy. When, at the end of his life, he was questioned on the realization of his ambitions, he said, 'he had done all that he meant to do, but he did not know whether it had been worth doing.'

Thomas Hardy and Sir Edmund Gosse
at Max Gate, Hardy's home near
Dorchester, 1927

Fleet Street and St Paul's Cathedral,
London, 1897

'Clubland' in the 1890s
St James Street, London

4

THE NOVELISTS MULTIPLY

I return now to that network of relationships into which Hardy and Stevenson were introduced when they joined the Savile Club. The lives of those who belonged to that circle had many connections, one of the most significant links being to Trinity College, Cambridge. Colvin had been at Trinity before moving to London, and in 1873 he was appointed to a professorship at Cambridge. Edmund Gosse lectured at Trinity, 1885–90. Trinity men were to be notable in the literature that would change the moral landscape of England. Bertrand Russell became a Fellow there in the 1890s, as did his friend George E. Moore. Moore's influential book on ethics included, by implication, a rejection of the Christian understanding of accountability to God and any absolute moral standard.[32] Five Trinity men founded the Midnight Society in 1899, and several of them joined the so-called Apostles, a secret society where Christian values were scoffed at and homosexuality approved.

Several of this clique, most notably Leonard Woolf and Lytton Strachey, were to combine with what became known as the Bloomsbury Group in London. Through thirty years the clever and witty Strachey would dominate the group. For the informal membership no beliefs were required, save agreement that Christianity was not the answer to the world's problems.

Many of the group became authors: Leonard Woolf controlled the literary pages of the *Spectator*; his wife, Virginia (daughter of Leslie Stephen), was a popular novelist; and Strachey set a new style in biographical writing with his faintly veiled sneers at Christians in his *Eminent Victorians*, published in 1918. Strachey's book was written when the First World War was still in progress: 'It proved itself far more destructive of the old British values than any legion of enemies. It was the instrument by which

[32] Moore's *Principia Ethica* (1903) was still a text book when I was a student at Durham in the early 1950s.

Strachey was able to "introduce the world to Moorism", becoming in the process the most influential writer of the Twenties.'[33] 'Our time will come about a hundred years hence', Strachey believed.

There were rivals for the fame of being the most influential writer in the 1920s, not least among whom were H. G. Wells and George Bernard Shaw. These were not Savile Club or Cambridge men, yet their lives intersected with the Bloomsbury Group at various points and no one was more adept at using novels and plays to advance the anti-Christian mission. Wells, like many others, began with contributions to monthly magazines. His novel, *Ann Veronica*, was turned down by Macmillan as 'exceedingly distasteful to the public that buys books published by our firm'. But it was published by Unwin in 1909. In the words of Wells' biographer, '*Ann Veronica* was a tract masquerading as a piece of romantic fiction. Had the plot not been so blatantly immoral by the standards of the day it would have been dismissed as banal, humourless and sentimental.'[34] Yet the popularity of Wells as an author rose rapidly. His

[33] Paul Johnson, *Modern Times: The World from the Twenties to the Eighties* (New York: Harper & Row, 1985), p. 169.

[34] Norman and Jeanne MacKenzie, *The Life of H. G. Wells, The Time Traveller* (London: Hogarth Press, 1987), p. 248.

Mr Britling Sees It Through, published in 1916, was said to have reached 'thirteen editions' before Christmas and brought in handsome American royalties. *A Short History of the World* (1920) ran to over two million copies in a few years, excluding numerous foreign translations. He concluded that what was needed for a better world was only a 'collective effort' to achieve 'a world order and one universal law and justice'. 'History becomes more and more a race between education and catastrophe.' In the late 1930s 'at least nineteen London publishers were carrying books by Wells in print'.

Despite his stance on morals, Wells was not averse to introducing some religion into his fiction. One of his books includes a 'conversion' to faith, and another describes how a bishop, abandoning traditional Christianity, recovered his soul by discovering 'the salvation of one human brotherhood under the rule of Righteousness: the Divine Will'. But underneath all this was Wells' abiding hostility to the evangelical belief of his mother. One writer speaks of how there was in his life a 'bitter, blasphemous denunciation of everything pertaining to God and the Lord Jesus'.[35] Certainly Wells had no intention of any relapse into

[35] Wilbur M. Smith, *Chats from a Minister's Library* (Boston: Wilde,1951), p. 187.

Christianity. Replying to a correspondent who had queried the 'religious phase' revealed in his books of the First World War period, he wrote:

> I wilfully tweaked the noses, and pulled the ears and generally insulted 'Christians' in order to wake them up to an examination of their religion. I'm not founding a new religion or looking for adherents.

The personal life of H. G. Wells was a parallel to his writing. He was looking for something he could never find: twice married ('I object to marriages as a general thing'), with numerous other temporary liasons, his life amounted to 'an endless search and repeated disappointments'. The closing words of his last book, *Mind at the End of Its Tether*, resonated with his own experience as well as with the world as he saw it:

> Our universe is not merely bankrupt; there remains no dividend at all; it has not simply liquidated; it is going clean out of existence, leaving not a wrack behind.

When a friend one day found him slumped in a chair and asked him what he was doing, he replied, 'Writing my epitaph.' Further asked what that would be, Wells replied, 'Quite short, just this—God damn you all: I told you so.' Yet this was the man whom the *New York Times* could describe as 'the greatest

public teacher of his day'; and whom, at his crem-
ation in 1946, J. B. Priestley eulogized as 'the great
prophet of our time'.

❧

George Bernard Shaw, in many ways a different
kind of man from Wells, served the same cause. He
was born in Dublin, and a satirical letter on Moody
and Sankey (when the evangelists visited that city
in 1875) was his first venture into print. His Prot-
estant relatives saw the letter as a public profession
of atheism. Shaw denied any such charge; he would
not even accept the title 'agnostic'. Indeed religion
would be prominent in a number of his later plays,
with characters represented as in search of God. But
it was a flippant search—had he not often said he
would give God five minutes to strike him dead? His
Black Girl in Search of God describes her failure in
meeting many theologies, and how she eventually
comes to a man Shaw intends us to recognize as Jesus
Christ. She 'finds him congenial and wise, but given
to conjuring tricks'. Christianity without the supernatural might be tolerable, but not a Christianity that
has God as its author. 'At present', Shaw declared,
'there is not a single credible established religion in

the world.'[36] 'Historical Christianity is largely a spent force . . . Jesus Christ has come down to earth. He is no longer an idol.'[37]

As with the whole coterie of his friends, Shaw believed evolution proved the slow progress of man to perfection. Salvation could be hoped for—as H. G. Wells also theorized—in supermen of the future. At the same time Shaw was for reforming society now. He was confident that socialism was the way forward, and he even came to believe that Soviet Communism under Stalin might show how the beautiful ideal could be realized. Supposedly the antagonist of myths, he embraced one of the darkest of the century. H. G. Wells was not far wrong in believing that Shaw 'lived in a world of make believe . . . He is an adolescent still at play.'[38] This was the man who, through his books, plays, and finally films, became described as 'Schoolmaster to the World'.[39] He was never happier than when he was changing

[36] *The Genius of Shaw*, ed. Michael Holroyd (New York: Holt, Rinehart and Winston, 1979), p. 88.

[37] Michael Holroyd, *Bernard Shaw: The Lure of Fantasy* (London: Chatto and Windus, 1991), p. 272.

[38] Michael Holroyd, *Bernard Shaw: The Pursuit of Power* (London: Chatto and Windus, 1989), p. 355.

[39] The words headed an obituary for Shaw in the *Saturday Review of Literature*.

the meaning of such words as 'wicked', 'marriage', 'life', and 'death'. Typical of his misuse of words was the assertion, 'I believe in life everlasting; but not for the individual.'

❧

I have mentioned Bertrand Russell above, as a Fellow of Trinity College, Cambridge, in the 1890s. A final place needs to be given to him in this brief overview of writers. A Victorian aristocrat, brought up by a Christian grandmother, he 'lost his faith' as a student at Trinity and found a new way forward in the writings of Henrik Ibsen and Walt Whitman.[40] The former taught him that 'self-realization' was man's first duty, and the latter showed that sexual desire had no necessary connection with morality. Shaw, Wells, and Edmund Gosse, had all preceded him as pupils of Ibsen, a Norwegian playwright who specialized in satirical social dramas. Wells's biographers make this significant comment:

> In 1891, in *The Quintessence of Ibsenism,* Shaw remarked that the implication of Ibsen's plays was

---

[40] In his *Familiar Studies of Men and Books* (1882), Stevenson has a chapter on Whitman and the misleading claim that he wrote in a spirit 'which I can only call one of ultra-Christianity'.

that it might be morally right to do things one's predecessors had thought infamous—right, that is to say, in terms of self-realisation, because moral emancipation was paramount over moral duty. It was that single thought, more than any other, that energized the shift from Victorian to Edwardian values.[41]

Russell's teaching role at Cambridge was interrupted in 1915 when he was removed from his Fellowship, then imprisoned in 1918 for a seditious article. He was reinstated at Trinity in 1919 but, apart from occasionally lecturing at the university and in other parts of the world, Russell was to earn his living by writing. Beginning in the 1890s, and continuing almost until his death in 1970 (a few months before his ninety-eighth birthday), there were to be over three thousand publications under his name. Some of his titles were on mathematics, a field where his brilliance had few equals, but the majority consisted of popular philosophy and social reform, in which role he was to dominate the twentieth century. The main problem he addressed was where certainty and happiness are to be found, given that man is 'an accident of evolution', and only 'a series of experiences'. His hopes lay in socialism and world

---

[41] N. and J. MacKenzie, *Wells,* p. 102.

government, and he was certain that Christianity was an obstacle to those hopes. In such titles as *Marriage and Morals, Religion and Science, Why I Am Not a Christian,* and *Has Religion Made Useful Contributions to Civilisation?* he showed plainly where he stood. Although disillusioned over his hopes before his death, he never returned to the Bible he had been taught in his childhood. 'I came to the conclusion', he could write, 'that the eternal world is trivial.' To a friend he could write: 'I am most anxious not to be thought to have any truck with Xtianity however emasculated—I want religion to die out, in schools and everywhere.'[42]

[42] Caroline Moorehead, *Bertrand Russell, A Life* (London: Sinclair-Stevenson, 1992), p. 345.

5

GENERAL LESSONS

1. If the question is asked, how a group of authors could produce such a change in the moral standards of a nation, it has to be said that it was done gradually and with a degree of deception. Stevenson had to be guarded in the opinions he made public, so much so that when he died in 1894, a fellow Scot and Presbyterian minister could write of him as 'a bright soul with faith in God and man'.[43] Even after the first volume of Stevenson's *Letters* appeared in 1899, with enough in it to dispute that claim, the representation continued in some quarters. W. E. Henley complained it was a 'barley-sugar effigy of the real man'.

[43] Ian Maclaren (a pseudonym for the Rev. John Watson).

The need for any writer of the 'progressive' school to exercise care and caution was demonstrated in the 1890s when one of Shaw's early plays, *Mrs Warren's Profession*, was banned by the Lord Chamberlain. It was the common belief of Wells, Shaw, and Russell that sexual relationships have no necessary connection with marriage but, when Wells was attacked in the press for advocating 'free love', he thought it necessary to respond with a denial. Russell challenged him on how he could deny in public what his friends all knew he affirmed in private, to which he replied, as his biographers report, 'that he had not yet saved enough money to live on the interest and that he did not propose to espouse free love openly until he could afford to do so'. It cannot be said that honesty ranked highly in the personal code of this group of men.

Dr Wilbur Smith, speaking in 1952, made this observation on the subject before us:

A few months ago, the *New York Times* issued a fifty-page brochure, four columns to a page, entitled 'A Century of Books', in which the editors gathered together reviews, appearing in this distinguished paper from 1851 to 1951, of one hundred and thirteen notable books, some of which continue to have world-wide influence, and a few, influence over millions. In carefully studying these pages, I am again impressed with the antichristian or non-christian position of the majority of these authors. In fact, apart from Hawthorne, I could not recognize one writer, man or woman, who could be called a believing Christian; and not one book among all those referred to here was written to extol Christian virtues, to honour the Lord Jesus, or to expound the Word of God. What can be the result of allowing these volumes to determine one's values but a hardening of the hearts of men against the Christian faith?[44]

2. It is commonly said that it was the progress of science in the Victorian era, and especially the teaching of evolution, that led to the setting aside of the Bible as revelation from God. Yet none of the men we have considered was a scientist (the fathers of Gosse and Stevenson were far better qualified in that area than were their sons). While the writings of Darwin, Herbert Spencer, or Huxley were made use of in defence of unbelief, they were not the commanding

[44] W. M. Smith, *The Minister and the Word of God, the Campbell Morgan Bible Lectureship* (London: Westminster Chapel, 1952), pp. 9–10. Smith quotes Clement C. J. Webb, 'The true enemy of religion in the modern world is not philosophy or science; it is the purely secular habit of mind.' *A Study of Religious Thought in England* (Oxford, 1933), pp. 185–6.

influence. That place belonged not to science, but to the hostility of the human heart to the holiness which the Bible reveals and requires. Unbelief springs from the desire that there be no authority to command our personal behaviour. The God who claims such authority must therefore be opposed. Equally, a salvation that includes submission to Christ as Lord has to be rejected. The exponents of this thinking never seem to have considered how very closely they resemble the character of the natural man revealed in Scripture: 'The mind that is set on the flesh is hostile to God; it does not submit to God's law, indeed it cannot' (*Rom.* 8:7).

Hostility to Christianity is sometimes explained and excused in terms of the Christian faith's allegedly poor representatives; one of Russell's set arguments was that Christianity has failed to make individuals virtuous. Yet the defence fails because it is to Christianity in its purest form that men are most antagonistic. 'Christianity without Christ' would have been acceptable to Stevenson, said his stepson; and it was Christ himself to whom such men as Shaw and Russell chiefly objected. But the advocates of unbelief rarely made that acknowledgement. They chose rather to present themselves as standing for 'knowledge' versus ignorance—the 'enlightened new' against the outworn old. The truth was rather that their moral state controlled their thinking. In the words of William Cowper's poem, *The Progress of Error*,

> Faults in the life breed errors in the brain,
> And these reciprocally those again.
> The mind and conduct mutually imprint
> And stamp their image in each other's mint.[45]

'All that men need is knowledge', was the claim, the assumption being that human nature will respond to truth. An advocate of that opinion once said that if only God were to reveal himself, all men would worship. That God has done this, and men crucified the Lord of glory, was not to be believed.

Yet even those who claim to have no knowledge of the existence of God can, at times, confess the very enmity towards him that is in their heart. Thus Stevenson, infatuated with Frances Sitwell, could write to her, 'I do not fear anything in life so long as you

---

[45] On the same point another has written: 'The success of error is owing chiefly to the state of mind into which it seeks entrance . . . if we suffer worldly lusts to obtain the mastery of reason and conscience,—we are in a fit state to welcome delusions, which may enable us in some measure to justify to ourselves a course on which inclination, not principle, has induced us to enter.' John Brown, *The Resurrection of Life: An Exposition of First Corinthians* xv (Edinburgh: Oliphant, 1866), p. 176.

are left to me, and this cursed God does not torment you too much.' Similarly when Russell thought he was suffering from cancer, he at once named 'God' as its author.

3. While the men we have considered were cautious, especially at first, in challenging Christian moral standards, they increasingly argued that they were presenting the kind of life that would make people truly happy and free. And they wanted people to think they were examples of their philosophy. Russell appeared to some people as a kind of 'Puritan'. Shaw was claimed as 'the last saint sent out from Ireland to save the world'.

Quoting this statement with approval, another writer continued: 'He was incorruptible. He never quarrelled. He took no offence. He bore no malice. He was without resentment.' Of Shaw's other 'virtues' his 'not drinking or smoking or eating meat' are listed.[46] This picture is close to the absurd. His contemporaries could speak very differently, and quarrelling there certainly was. When Bertrand Russell's wife, with his concurrence, accused Shaw of being 'frivolous and cruel', Shaw replied by telling

[46] *Genius of Shaw*, p. 91.

her that her husband was a tyrant. H. G. Wells called Shaw an 'unmitigated moral Victorian ass'. Rebecca West, another novelist of the Bloomsbury Group, described Shaw as 'a eunuch perpetually inflamed by flirtation'.[47]

Russell sought to fend off discussion of his sexual morality by scoffing at the Christian's 'morbid interest in sex'. The truth is that the lives of none of these men (excluding Stevenson after his marriage) will stand examination when it comes to relations with the opposite sex. They all believed and practised what they called 'open marriage'. Russell and Wells had a multiplicity of relationships, in, out of, and along with marriage. And their lives show that sexual immorality never stands alone. Dishonesty is its companion. When Russell's third wife was accused by a friend of heartlessness in divorcing him, she replied, as Caroline Moorehead writes:

> She had just discovered, from 'independent sources', how Russell had told people that he disliked her intensely, and had done so for years. She commented it was in his nature to loathe people but pretend to their faces that he liked them. 'By talking against each to each he has always put everyone against everyone

47 Victoria Glendinning, *Rebecca West, A Life* (London; Phoenix, 1998), p. 38.

else among his intimates, and with women it is dread-
ful, he collects several at a time who each believes
that he loves her and hates the others.'[48]

The claim that the progressives were admirers of a
better morality was one of the great falsehoods of history. Love for all the world was a maxim they taught
as the way to world peace. But love for individuals,
and peace in their lives, were conspicuously absent.[49]
The moral code to be found in 'self-realization' was,
in reality, no more than the love of self: the 'good'
was whatever the heart desired. 'I am the captain of
my soul', was the yardstick. After Stevenson's death,
Henley made this criticism of his character:

> At bottom Stevenson was an excellent fellow. But he
> was of his essence what the French call *personnel*. He
> was, that is, incessantly and passionately interested
> in Stevenson.[50]

We have noted Emma Hardy making the very same
comment on her husband. According to the Bible
this is not a blot applicable only to a few: it applies
to all as we are by nature. 'All seek their own, not
the things that are Jesus Christ's' (*Phil.* 2:21). The

---

[48] Moorehead, *Bertrand Russell*, p. 490.

[49] Russell 'never gave his heart to anyone'. K. Tait, *My Father
Bertrand Russell* (London: Gollancz, 1976).

[50] Harman, *Stevenson*, p. 462.

real problem that this school of men could not solve, either in their own lives or in those of others, was human nature. Wells, characteristically selfish himself, spoke the truth when he corrected Shaw in 1941 for 'assuming man is a rational being, whereas he is nothing of the sort'.[51]

4. I have claimed above that the writers—many of them novelists—played a major part in the demoralization of Britain. A common answer to that charge has been that 'words' can have no such effect on behaviour. The novelist, it is said, 'is only portraying life as it is'.[52]

[51] MacKenzie, *Wells,* p. 431.
[52] The defence that the new type of novels was 'portraying life as it is' was popular in France where impure fiction was already commonplace. In the 1880s the French historian, M. de Pressensé, complained of a stream of writing that was 'simply an incentive to debauchery'. 'Zola and his followers of the so-called Realistic-school, have degraded the high office of the littérateur by corrupting the public mind.' Translations of such French authors were spreading in England at this date, despite a London publisher being prosecuted in the Central Criminal Court in October 1888. In Parliament the Government promised to use the law to check the circulation of impure literature, but there was a momentum that legal action would not stop. As a London newspaper commented, publishers were seeing the financial profit in gaining a wider market for fiction with lowered moral standards: 'We can hardly wonder that publishers, more enterprising than scrupulous, when they see tales of vice

It was along such lines that Stevenson replied to his father's protest against irreverence included in a play he had written with Henley: 'Religion is in the world; I do not think you are the man to deny the importance of its role', he wrote.

So the play included a confrontation between a blackguard and an evangelical, with language supposedly appropriate. He might agree, RLS went on, that the writing was poorly done and in that respect a failure, but, 'Concern yourself about no failure; they do not cost lives, as in engineering . . . do not think of it; if the writer means well and tries hard, no failure will injure him, whether with God or man.'[53]

Thomas Stevenson knew differently. Words can be dangerous, as even the Greek poets were aware: 'Be not deceived: evil communications corrupt good

---

and crime, or murder, forgery, and seduction, eagerly devoured by the educated classes, easily blind themselves to the wrong they are committing by supplying similar to a different class of palates. A vitiated taste in fiction, and, to some extent in poetry too, has been visible in English society for many years past, and novel writers of great ability and power of imagination have not hesitated to minister to it.' [Quoted from 'Bad Reading, and Those Who Provide It', in *The Sword and the Trowel*, ed. C. H. Spurgeon (London: Passmore and Alabaster, 1889), pp. 6–7. See also p. 444.]

[53] *Letters of Robert Louis Stevenson*, ed. S. Colvin, vol. 1 (London: Methuen, 1911), p. 336.

manners' (*1 Cor.* 15:33). A description of the disso-
lute, and their irreverent language, *does* injure. Nor
is it even necessary for literature to be specifically
immoral to have this effect. Books that constantly
convey a purely secular mindset, that treat the
present world as though it were the only world, that
studiously avoid truths revealed in Scripture (unless
to scoff)—such books impart a godless view of life,
and teach their readers to regard this world as the
only 'reality'.

Examined by the claim that they were advocates
of greater human happiness, these men were all
tragic failures. 'There is no doubt', writes one of his
biographers, 'that though he tried to keep it secret,
the last three years of Stevenson's life were deeply
unhappy.'[54] Stevenson himself went as far as saying
in a letter of 1891 (referring to months in 1883), 'I
was only once happy.' One of Russell's favourite
subjects for a popular lecture was happiness, in which
he argued that 'it was perfectly possible for man to be
happy, provided he took the right steps'. His hearers
little knew how the speaker's own life contradicted
the argument. Russell destroyed the happiness of
successive wives. In a moment of truthfulness he

---

[54] Harman, *Stevenson*, p. 450.

once wrote, 'I always bring misery to anyone who has anything to do with me.' In the words of one of his mistresses, he was a man 'passing from person to person, never giving any real happiness—or finding any.'[55] A similar verdict was applicable to H. G. Wells. His biographers say his life confirms 'the manner in which a man who combines messianic truth in himself with the habits of a philanderer produces havoc in the lives of all around him'.[56]

One characteristic of the non-Christian life is very conspicuous in all these men and women who lived for themselves. Selfishness leads irresistibly to loneliness, as individuals turn in on themselves. Russell spoke of 'so many lonely years', and the evidence is there in most of the biographies of these men, not least as they approached what they claimed to be their 'extinction'. Rebecca West at the end, 'could not bear to be alone'. The death of Virginia Woolf was perhaps the saddest of all. Not long before that event, the son of her friend and 'lover', Vita Sackville-West, wrote to her that all the writings of the Bloomsbury Group had achieved nothing:

[55] Ray Monk, *Bertrand Russell, The Spirit of Solitude* (London: Jonathan Cape, 1996), p. 607.
[56] MacKenzie, *Wells*, p. 455.

'Bloomsbury, it seemed to him, had been living in a fool's paradise enjoying cultivated pleasures while it neglected the first duty of the intellectual, which is to save the world from its follies.'[57] But Virginia Woolf had learned that it was beyond the power of all their brilliant intellects to 'save the world', and in March 1941, her pockets filled with stones, she drowned herself in the River Ouse at the age of 59. Gertrude Himmelfarb had reason to write of the novelists who came from this school that they were 'in general an intellectual community suffering a larger proportion of nervous breakdowns, it would seem, than almost any other'.[58]

But even when the effect of the false teaching could be seen, it did not change the determination of the promoters. Russell tried to put a number of his principles into practice. For five years from 1927 he gave much of his life to Beacon Hill School which he had founded. It was to be a working exhibition of his ideals. There was no 'authority' (a dirty word),

---

[57] *Virginia Woolf, A Biography* (London: Hogarth Press, 1990), p. 220. Yet, while Bloomsbury did not 'save the world from its follies', Paul Johnson can write: 'The influence of Bloomsbury had reached upwards and downwards by the 1930s to embrace almost the entire political nation.' *Modern Times*, p. 347.
[58] *Victorian Minds*, p. 219

no punishments, no taboos, no 'sexual repression'. 'National history' was rejected, nudity was encouraged, and teachers were allowed to have affairs among themselves (Russell's own wife was to use that liberty and bear someone else's child). No school, or society, with such a basis could survive, and in the 1930s Russell had to confess that the experiment had been a mistake. Thereafter 'he was reluctant to discuss the school with anyone who came to see him'. One former pupil was to say of her experience at Beacon Hill, 'It smashed my bright world of happiness, and left me to spend the rest of my life searching for a replacement.'

I have written of individual lives that ended in sorrow but the outcome has been tragedy on a much greater scale. For the full outworking of the ideas of these writers, we have noted Strachey looking to 'about a hundred years hence'. What he anticipated with pleasure, some regarded with dismay. W. R. Inge wrote of the effects that Russell's philosophy would have upon the nation:

No God. No country. No family. Refusal to serve in war. Free love. More play. Less work. No punishments. Go as you please. It is difficult to imagine any programme which, if carried out, would be more utterly ruinous to a country situated as Great Britain today.[59]

Before the end of the twentieth century the full harvest of which Inge had spoken was to be seen in Britain. His words had needed no prophetic insight, for the effects of paganism upon a people have long been a matter of history. What we have today is a rerun of life as it was in Rome in the first century:

> Marriage had fallen into deeper and deeper contempt. The freedom of single life was preferred by both sexes. Seneca went so far as to affirm that marriage was only contracted in order that adultery might afford additional charm, and declared that whoever had no love affairs was to be despised. Unnatural vices prevailed . . . In such a state of society, even if marriages were celebrated, the children were few in number. They were not desired in advance and they were not welcomed when they appeared. As there was no sense of the sacredness of human life infanticide was commonly practised. The destruction

---

[59] Moorehead, *Russell*, p. 382. Others gave similar warning. The Bishop of Rochester, while speaking of Russell as 'the greatest brain of his generation', asked him to consider the 'untold misery' he would bring upon young people who followed his ideas on sex.

of unborn children was even more practised than infanticide, and not only did moral disintegration ensue in the destruction of family life, but the very foundations of the state were undermined in the decrease of the native population.[60]

Sin prevails, despite its consequences. Unbelief, far from being the result of superior knowledge, is irrational. It succeeds because of the power that leads men and women to love darkness rather than light. Jesus Christ alone is greater than that power. There is no sin he cannot forgive; no depravity he cannot remove; no human heart he cannot change. Psalm 107 describes the very kind of human history that I have reported in these pages, but the last word is not one of gloom:

> Because they rebelled against the words of God, and contemned the counsel of the most High: therefore he brought down their heart with labour; they fell down, and there was none to help. Then they cried unto the LORD in their trouble, and he saved them out of their distresses. He brought them out of darkness and the shadow of death, and brake their bands in sunder. Oh that men would praise the LORD for

---

[60] David R. Breed, *A History of the Preparation of the World for Christ* (New York: Fleming Revell, 1893), pp. 426-7.

his goodness, and for his wonderful works to the children of men!

The words of Anna Ölander state the alternatives which face us all:

If I gained the world but lost the Saviour,
Were my life worth living for a day?
Could my yearning heart find rest and comfort
In the things that soon must pass away?
If I gained the world, but lost the Saviour,
Would my gain be worth the life-long strife?
Are all earthly pleasures worth comparing
For a moment with a Christ-filled life?

Had I wealth and love in fullest measure,
And a name revered both far and near,
Yet no hope beyond, no harbour waiting
Where my storm-tossed vessel I could steer—
If I gained the world, but lost the Saviour,
Who endured the cross and died for me,
Could then all the world afford a refuge,
Whither in my anguish I might flee?

O what emptiness without the Saviour,
Mid the sins and sorrow here below!
And eternity, how dark without Him—
Only night and tears and endless woe!

What though I might live without the Saviour,
When I come to die, how would it be?
O to face the valley's gloom without Him!
And without Him all eternity!

O the joy of having all in Jesus!
What a balm the broken heart to heal!
Ne'er a sin so great but He'll forgive it,
Nor a sorrow that He does not feel!
If I have but Jesus, only Jesus,
Nothing else in all the world beside
O then everything is mine in Jesus—
For my needs and more He will provide.

PART TWO

Men are so absorbed in the affairs of the world that God, the Supreme Reality, seems unreal to them. When that which is least real is everything, that which is most real appears to be nothing.

The Christ who once died now lives and reigns. The Holy Spirit, whom He sends to believing hearts, is the connecting link between our faith-experience and the historical foundation of our faith. Without the Cross and Resurrection, there would be no Christian experience at all. The historical facts make the experience possible, while the experience verifies the facts. Christian experience is the final apologetic of the Christian faith.

Daniel Lamont
The Anchorage of Life

A girl holding in her right hand a stylus and in her left a wax tablet.

A youth reading a papyrus roll. The original New Testament documents were written on papyrus; a fragment of John's Gospel, dating from the first half of the second century, is among copies that survive.

Illustrations from Barré's *Herculaneum*

6

IS CHRISTIANITY FICTION?

In the eighteenth century an actor was once asked by a preacher why the theatre was so full while the church was so empty. The answer was this: 'Simply because we act fiction as if it were fact; whereas you preach fact as though it were fiction.'

But supposing the opinion becomes accepted that Christianity is fiction, what then? For some it would not matter a great deal. They think the Christian tradition retains a moral value regardless of its origin. Religious ideals, they suppose, do not need an historical foundation to be appreciated or practised. While such an argument may be true of some religions, it does not fit Christianity.

Christianity claims that God has revealed himself at a point in history, in the person of his Son, Jesus

Christ, whose life, death and resurrection are now recorded for all to read. To Jesus Christ and his words, Christianity claims, all people owe the obedience that they owe to God. Its message of salvation is about meeting Jesus Christ and experiencing his love and resurrection power. Christians are people with a living relationship with Christ; he is the one they mean to honour and obey. In a real sense, they are no longer their own, they belong to Christ. So if Christianity were not true its message would fall and become meaningless. Indeed, according to the New Testament, there would be no message at all. In the words of Paul (one of the earliest teachers of Christianity), 'If Christ be not risen, then is our preaching vain, and your faith is also vain' (*1 Cor.* 15:14). Is Christianity fiction? The question is of fundamental importance.

We take up the question with this observation: if Christianity is fiction there has to be a period in time, at least an approximate date, when it was invented.

What about AD 200, or thereabouts, as a possible date? That is clearly impossible, because by that date the Christian message was spread right across the Roman world, from Spain to Egypt, probably even to Britain in the west as well as far to the east.

By AD 200 the teaching also existed in many written documents and statements; some of them even carved on the walls of catacombs in Rome.

If invention it was, the date for the origin of Christianity has to be much earlier than AD 200. At this point non-Christian sources can help us. A letter exists, for instance, from AD 112, written by Pliny, Roman governor of Bithynia and Pontus (a large part of present-day northern Turkey). In this letter Pliny reports to the Emperor Trajan on many affected by Christianity in his region. He describes Christians as people who 'were wont, on an appointed day, to meet before it was light, and to sing with one another, an hymn to Christ as God'.

Another non-Christian source tells us how numerous Christians were in the capital of the Roman Empire at a still earlier date. Tacitus, the Roman historian, writes of how, to divert attention from the possibility of his own responsibility for the burning of Rome in AD 64, the Emperor Nero singled out Christians and

> punished them with the most exquisite sufferings. The author of that sect was Christ, who, in the reign of Tiberius, was punished with death by the procurator Pontius Pilate. But the pestilent superstition,

which, for the present, was suppressed, broke out afresh, not only in Judea, where the evil first began, but in the city [i.e., Rome] . . . First, then, those who confessed were apprehended; next, by their information, a vast multitude who were convicted, not so much of the burning, as of the hatred of mankind. These were made a sport of in their death.

No one has questioned the basic facts alleged by Tacitus. His assertion on the unpopularity of Christianity in Rome in AD 64 agrees with what the first Christian history—the *Acts of the Apostles*—also reports. Paul, in Rome about the year AD 61, found that Christians were 'a sect everywhere spoken against' (*Acts* 28:22).[1]

The information given by Pliny and Tacitus on the spread of Christianity shows that for the faith to have become established so widely at these early dates, its origin—whether true or fictitious—must

---

[1] Evidently a misrepresentation of Christianity was widespread. Contrary to reports he had heard, Pliny discovered 'that the rites of the Christian religion were simple and harmless, that their disciples forbade all crimes, that the worshippers bound themselves by a *sacramentum* to do no wrong, and that the charges commonly brought against them of practising child murder, cannibalism, and other hideous offences at their private meetings were groundless.' I quote from W. M. Ramsay, *The Church in the Roman Empire* (London: Hodder and Stoughton, 1894), p. 205.

have occurred close to the time of Christ himself. The relevance of this to the main question will appear below. It is true that the Greek and Roman world was the scene of many myths and legends. It is true, also, that to create the fictitious is no great problem. It happens all the time. But I hope to show that to invent such a fiction as Christianity would involve a very great problem indeed.

Consider how the disciples of the New Testament presented the message which they called all to believe. About what that message was there can be no mistake. Their argument hung on one simple point. It was that Jesus of Nazareth is 'the Christ'. They placed the reliability of everything else they said on that one assertion. Today the connection of the name of 'Jesus' with 'Christ' is so commonplace as to seem inconsequential. Is it not just a question of words? Far from it! For the Jews of the first century the identification of Jesus with Christ was earthshaking.

To understand why this was so, it has first to be remembered that what we call the Old Testament Scriptures had been completed and were in circulation hundreds of years before the Christian era. They were constantly read by the Jews, and from that source came the expectation of the 'Messiah' who was to come. The title in Hebrew means 'Anointed one', and the equivalent word in Greek is 'Christ'. It was by anointing that Old Testament kings were set apart for their office, being a symbol of divine qualification for their work. For a greater work than that of kings, the Old Testament promised, a future Deliverer would be 'anointed'. He would be 'higher than the kings of the earth' (*Psa.* 89:27). 'All kings shall fall down before him: all nations shall serve him' (*Psa.* 72:11). His would be no temporary reign. His kingdom would never pass away, 'it shall stand for ever' (*Dan.* 2:44). 'His name shall endure for ever' (*Psa.* 72:17).

To him belong divine power and glory because he is God (*Isa.* 9:6). So, although throughout the Old Testament the command of God is to put no trust in man, concerning the Messiah all are commanded to put their trust in him (*Psa.* 2:12). 'Whosoever will not hearken unto my words which he [the Messiah] shall speak in my name, I will require it of him' (*Deut.* 18:15).

This promised Messiah, or Christ, was the recurring theme of the Scriptures given to the Jews. Born of woman, he is first announced as the one who is to undo the devastation that sin and Satan have brought on the human race (*Gen.* 3:15); with increasing clearness his family line is traced through Abraham, through Judah, and through David. His place of birth is named as Bethlehem (*Mic.* 5:2); and the place and manner of his death are also named (*Dan.* 9:26). The Messiah's sufferings and death will be the God-appointed means for the forgiveness of sins. Thus the prophet Isaiah writes:

> But he was pierced through for our transgressions,
> He was crushed for our iniquities;
> The chastening for our well-being fell upon him,
> And by his scourging we are healed.
> All of us like sheep have gone astray,
> Each of us has turned to his own way;
> But the Lord has caused the iniquity of us all
> To fall on him (*Isa.* 53:5–6).

From other Old Testament prophets the message is the same. The book of Daniel says that Messiah would come 'to finish the transgression, to make an end of sins, and to make reconciliation for iniquity' (*Dan.* 9:24). And while these promises were revealed to the Jewish people, this is not nationalistic triumphalism. The promises are for the whole world. As far back as the time of Abraham, God promised that in his offspring 'shall all the nations of the earth be blessed' (*Gen.* 22:18). 'Men shall be blessed in him: all nations shall call him blessed' (*Psa.* 72:17).

Here, then, is the reason why for the Jews of the first-century the identification of Jesus of Nazareth with the Christ was earthshaking. If it were true that Jesus of Nazareth was 'the Christ', then the Son of God had come; the Messianic age—the promised turning point in history had arrived. The faith of the first disciples was expressed in the words of Simon Peter, 'You are the Christ, the Son of the living God' (*Matt.* 16:16); and after Christ's resurrection that same confession was to be the substance of all their preaching. They claimed that everything concerning the Messiah, detailed beforehand in the Old Testament, they had *seen* fulfilled in Jesus. They spoke of 'That which was from the beginning, which we have heard, which we have seen with our eyes, which we have looked upon, and our hands have handled' (*1 John* 1:1).

As recorded in the book of the *Acts of the Apostles*, the message 'Jesus is the Christ!' was repeated everywhere: in Jerusalem, 'God has made that same Jesus, whom you have crucified, both Lord and Christ' (*Acts* 2:36); in Damascus, 'Straightway he preached Christ in the synagogues, that he is the Son of God' (9:20); in Caesarea, 'Him God raised up the third day . . . To him give all the prophets witness' (10:40, 43); in Thessalonica, 'this Jesus whom I preach unto you is Christ' (17:3); again at Corinth (18:5, 28); and finally at Rome, 'persuading them concerning Jesus, both out of the law of Moses, and out of the prophets, from morning till evening' (28:23).

Now this raises a new aspect to the question, Is Christianity fiction? If what the disciples claimed to be true of Jesus was all to be found in a book written long before he was born [the Old Testament], the idea of a fictitious invention is narrowed to only two possibilities. As I have said, the Old Testament record was completed some hundreds of years before the first century AD. But could it be that Christians 'edited' the Old Testament manuscripts, adding details of what really only happened in their own lifetime? This is impossible for a simple reason: the Old Testament was never an exclusively Christian preserve. It was jealously guarded by Jews who never became Christians. Large parts of the Prophets they knew by heart, and their scribes scrupulously watched over every word. So if any fraud in the transmission of the text had ever occurred it would have been speedily discovered and repudiated. There was no such discovery. The Jews had various objections to Christianity, but an allegation of rewriting Old Testament Scriptures was never one of them.

One other possibility remains. What if the first disciples fabricated their story to make it match the record of the Prophets? Could they have composed a fictitious life of Jesus in order to harmonize it with the prophetic records? Here is where the time-frame element becomes especially relevant. Consider the dates that we know. Tacitus identified the crucifixion of Christ as having taken place in the reign of the Emperor Tiberius, when Pontius Pilate was governor of Judea. It is certain that Pilate was governor between AD 26 and 36. From Christian sources we can be more explicit, and place the death of Christ around the year AD 30.[2]

---

[2] The New Testament dates the work of John the Baptist, the forerunner of Christ, as beginning 'in the fifteenth year of the reign of Tiberius Caesar', which is best understood in our calendar as referring to the year AD 26. The Messianic work of Jesus began shortly after the preaching of John, and continued for some three and a half years.

The probability is that Christ's ministry began towards the end of the year 26, and that the first Passover of his public work was in AD 27. This would agree with a date, given by those who were not disciples who were present at that Passover in Jerusalem; they spoke of the Temple as being in the process of building for 46 years (*John* 2:20). As the date for the start of the building of this Temple is known, 46 years later would make the date AD 27. Some of the most striking confirmations of the reliability of the New Testament records lie in such seemingly incidental references.

Now, we have seen that the Christian message was widespread across the Mediterranean before AD 64 (when Christians were numerous in Rome). This means that, if the message were fiction, it would need to have been established many years earlier; the date could not have been long after the death of Christ, only some 34 years earlier. In other words, the events of which Christians spoke and wrote belonged to a period familiar to many thousands in Judea.

Here is where the invention of myth diverges so markedly from the origins of Christianity. For fiction to be accepted as truth, its allegations must be set in remote places, or in distant times, inaccessible for checking. But the Christian message about Christ appealed to events public, recent, and well known. The life and death of Christ, far from being witnessed only by an inner circle, had been seen by large numbers in Judea and Galilee. A make-believe 'life' was impossible. This is one reason the message carried the conviction that it did. The appeal of the disciples was to contemporary history. Paul, on trial before Festus and King Agrippa (c. AD 59), could say about Christ, 'The king knows of these things, before whom also I speak freely: for I am persuaded that none of these things are hidden from him; for this thing was not done in a corner' (*Acts* 26:26).

Knowledge about Christ was so widespread that Paul was sure King Agrippa was bound to have heard it. The Jews who were contemporaries of the first disciples did not dispute that the life of Christ was history. As one commentator says on the verse just quoted: 'All that was said about Jesus was transacted in the very capital of the nation, and the Sanhedrin and the procurator Pilate were involved, and Jesus was a national figure, whose fame filled even the surrounding lands' (R. C. H. Lenski). A fabricated life and crucifixion designed to fit the Old Testament prophecies is impossible.[3]

The only credible explanation of the perfect match between the Messiah of the Old Testament and Jesus Christ is the one given in Scripture. God planned a way of salvation; he announced it beforehand, and brought it to pass in a manner that left the disciples themselves amazed.

---

[3] An example of how the Gospels provide verifiable material is in Matthew 27:3–8. We are there told of the remorse of Judas who, after his betrayal of Jesus, returned the money he had been paid to the Chief Priests. With that money they bought a field: 'That field was called, the field of blood, unto this day.' Matthew's Gospel was written for Jews, some of whom could readily have checked the derivation of this name. The words were obviously written before Jerusalem was razed to the ground in AD 70 by the Romans.

There are other arguments against the possibility that Christianity was a Jewish invention that originated in the 30s of the first century AD. What motive, we might ask, could lead men and women to collude together to impose a falsehood of this nature? It brought them nothing that human nature desires—no worldly advancement or material benefit, no praise from their own race. Instead three centuries of sufferings marked the beginning of the Christian church. But this was an argument too inferior for the disciples to employ. Their case rested on the Person of Christ himself—his character, his words, his death and resurrection. The accounts found in the four Gospels (Matthew, Mark, Luke, and John) were written by different men. In one thing they are identical. They describe Jesus as living and acting as no one else had ever done. Could such a Person be their own invention?

So far is the portrayal of the character and work of Christ above human devising that the very possibility can scarcely be conceived. What we see in Christ transcends humanity. Many have repeated the words of the Jewish temple guards, 'Never man spoke like this man' (*John* 7:46); still more have said with Thomas, 'My Lord and my God!'

(*John* 20:28). One who studied Christ wrote this cogent summary:

> He knew the unknowable: the human heart and all things;
> He loved the unlovable: the human sinner;
> He did the impossible: he died and rose again;
> He was the impossible: a sinless character.

With good reason it has been said that in a country untouched by Christianity, it would be morally impossible for anyone to conceive of such a character, morally and religiously, as that of Jesus Christ. That same impossibility existed in the first century.

And yet all this is not enough to make anyone a Christian. The evidence for the message, firm though it is, can do no more than win attention, and that perhaps only temporarily. It cannot of itself gain a response. Were this not so, all Judea would have become Christian in the first century. The problem with which Christianity has to deal is far deeper than a matter of intellectual persuasion; and Jesus prepared his disciples for this when he foretold, 'Neither will they be persuaded, though one rise from the dead' (*Luke* 16:31). After his death and resurrection, and with Old Testament prophecy fulfilled before their eyes, the Jews, as a people, still did not believe. As Paul told his hearers in a synagogue: 'They that dwell at Jerusalem, and their rulers, because they knew him not, nor yet the voices of the prophets, which are read every Sabbath day, they have fulfilled them in condemning him' (*Acts* 13:27). Unbelief reigns in human nature with a power that facts alone cannot displace. The message of submission to Christ, of turning from self to the living God and his commandments, is utterly uncongenial. 'Men loved darkness rather than light, because their deeds were evil' (*John* 3:19).

If this biblical account of human nature is true, it leads to an arresting question: How is the extraordinary confidence of the first Christian disciples to be explained? Why did they not find their mission utterly impossible and depressing? The only answer that makes sense is the one given by the New Testament. Christianity succeeds by supernatural power. The first disciples did not find Christ; he found them, forgave them, changed them. From the time they met him after his resurrection they believed he was present to give new life wherever his word went. All their assurance was in him. From this came a startling claim in their preaching, and one of vital relevance for us. The New Testament teaches that the Christian faith is verifiable anywhere, and at any time, because Christ lives now to make himself known. He will meet all who, acknowledging their sins, come to him in repentance and faith. The 'good news' at the centre of Christianity is that what God promised in the Old Testament he has now fulfilled (*Rom.* 1:2). Christ has done for sinners what they could never do for themselves—in their place he obeyed God's holy law and in their place he suffered the penalty of sin, which is death. What we deserved has not come to us: it came to him; and now all that belongs to him is freely given to us. Therefore for those who trust in Christ there is 'no condemnation'. They are counted by God as having done all that Jesus did in their place; they are 'justified [declared righteous] by his blood' (*Rom.* 5:9). A changed life follows faith in Christ, but it does not contribute anything to our acceptance with God. That has been accomplished by Christ alone: salvation comes freely to those deserving nothing: 'For by grace are you saved through faith; and that not of yourselves: it is the gift of God. Not of works lest any man should boast' (*Eph.* 2:8–9).

Christianity is history but we do not become Christians by believing in history. Rather there is a present invitation from Christ himself to be answered. And there is a promise he is ready to make real: 'The one who comes to me I will by no means cast out . . . If any man will do his will, he shall know of the doctrine whether it be of God, or whether I speak of myself' (*John* 6:37; 7:36). These words are conditional on our bringing nothing to Christ except the awareness of our need of him. Because the Son of God is the same, salvation and Christian experience are as near to us as they were to the first disciples.

All who trust in him will find *certainty*, not fiction: 'Most assuredly, I say to you, he who hears my word and believes in him who sent me has everlasting life, and shall not come into judgment, but has passed from death into life' (*John* 5:24).

INDEX